This guidebook  *...rgh*
from the eyes o... *...d*
attend school the... *...ook,*
it's a creative boo... ...offers an alternative look
at this amazing town. It is brimming with fun ideas
to spend an afternoon.

We hope you enjoy it.

Journey Through Musselburgh

an unofficial local guide

SUPER POWER BOOKS

Guidebook class

People of Musselburgh

Loads of famous people are from Musselburgh like Callum Beatie and John Clarke and also politicians.

There is a difference between people in Edinburgh and Musselburgh. It's less scary in Musselburgh too. For instance, there are always loads of fireworks in Edinburgh and they probably upset the dogs. Musselburgh is much more peaceful and quiet.

Musselburgh has various celebrations throughout the year. These include a duck race along the River Esk, where people bring plastic ducks to race. The town also selects representatives called the Honest Lad and Lassie. Those selected represent the values and beliefs of the 'Honest Town', Musselburgh's nickname.

Section One

Places of Interest

Historical parts of Musselburgh

Written by Ashton, Harrison and Martin

Roman Archer Statue
Mall Ave, Musselburgh EH21

The Bow and Arrow Statue is located at the River Esk next to the Roman Bridge. Its real name is 'The Musselburgh Archer'. The archer represents the Roman occupation of the area during the year 80 A.D. It's also a symbol of the Battle of Pinkie Cleugh that took place in 1547. It also represents the Musselburgh Silver Arrow Competition and Trophy.

The man doesn't have an arrow in his bow in the statue, but what is cool is that there are lots of arrows around Musselburgh so you can see if you can find them all. Some of them are in the walls of buildings, like the archer has shot arrows.

It has a very good review on Tripadvisor.

It's good because it is free and you can go and see it whenever you want. So on a day you're walking along the River Esk, you could see if you can find it.

Musselburgh Library

10 Bridge St, Musselburgh EH21 6AG

Opening times: Mon and Thur - 9am-7pm Tue and Fri - 9am -5pm, Wed 10-5, Sat 10-4, Sun - closed

The Musselburgh Library is a warm and safe place to visit. It is located at 10 Bridge Street, Musselburgh. The library has excellent service and a 4.8 star Google review. The staff are welcoming and friendly and attend to all your needs.

It is quite small but cosy and has a big selection of books and DVDs. And all for a cheap price too!

They also host regular events, including a book club, BookBug sessions, Dungeons and Dragons, computer basics classes and a Lego club. Not only that, they also provide a massive variety of services such as disabled access,  doggy bags, free wi-fi, foodbank and 10 public access computers. You can also print in colour there. Just loads of useful things.

The university was named after the Scottish Queen, Queen Margaret.

Queen Margaret University

Queen Margaret University Way Musselburgh EH21 6UU

Queen Margaret University (or QMU as it's known) was founded in 1875. The best part of the university is that there are lots of sports you can play, including basketball, football, badminton and there is also a gym. Anyone can use their facilities as long as you pay. If you want to go to the gym, you can pay £5 for a pass and you can go for the whole weekend. We think that's really reasonable and cheaper than the sports centre in Musselburgh (also in this book).

The university was named after the Scottish Queen, Queen Margaret.

If you enrol at QMU, you can study Business Management, Drama, Film and Media, Nursing, Psychology and many more. There are about 3500 undergraduates who go there. There are other universities in Edinburgh, but this is the only one in Musselburgh.

The new building only opened in 2007. We're 50/50 about whether we think the building looks good. Inside there is a cafe, student union, places to sit and chill or work and rooms you have lectures in.

We asked the people in the class whether they would want to go to the university. Eight people said yes and five people said no. But the no people might just be because they would want to live with someone else.

Roman Bridge
River Esk Path, Inveresk
Musselburgh EH21 7UA

The Roman Bridge is an old bridge created by the Romans to get over the River Esk. It was built in 1300 and was knocked down. The one that stands now was built in 1597. It was used by the English to escape the Battle of Bannockburn in 1314.

We feel quite neutral about the bridge, but it helps us get over the river. It does look quite nice, though.

It has got 4.5 stars on Tripadvisor, so you should check it out.

War Memorial

The War Memorial is an old High Street fountain, which was restored and converted. It cost £58,000. Dedicatory plaques are placed on the sides of the fountain and the area around it has been landscaped. There are 203 names on the memorial. It used to be a functioning water fountain in WWII. It was unveiled in 2000 and is made of metal, bronze, stone and sandstone. We think it looks good and it's nice to have a name plaque to remember people.

Buntan Theatre

Ladywell Way, Musselburgh EH21 6AA

The Brunton Theatre is right on the High Street in Musselburgh and it is across the road from the Library (also talked about in this book). Inside there is a cafe so you can eat before you watch one of their great shows!

From personal experience the shows are good and they include the audience in some of them.

They have shows like 'Enough of Him', 'My Old School' and 'Sinbad the Pantomime'.

They have a good car park so you can usually get a parking space. Tickets are reasonable too. Sometimes they start at £15 per person, which we think is good.

Section Two

Sports

For the sports fans

Written by Lewis and Manpreet

Musselburgh Golf Course
Monktonhall, Musselburgh
Edinburgh EH21 6SA

If you are interested in golf this is the perfect golf course as it is an 18 hole course that is really good!

It has very historic origins and you can learn a lot from the locals. It is one of the oldest golf courses on the planet and dates back to the 1400s. It is the oldest golf course in the world

There are events and tournaments for people who think they can win prizes or money

Musselburgh golf club charges £40 a year for a membership. The opening times for the course is 9am - 9pm.

There is no driving range but you can practice on a putting green.

There is no age limit to play golf there.
You can hire golf clubs there if you don't have your own. You can also hire golf buggies to get around the course.

Musselburgh Racecourse has a great history! It has been there for 206 years.

Musselburgh Racecourse
Linkfield Rd, Musselburgh EH21 7RE

You should go to the racecourse as it has great races and food to enjoy. If you're interested in horse racing it would be a great day out. It is pretty famous too.

It is quite expensive but the food is really good and there's a big variety of and if you like alcohol there is also a bar inside.

Musselburgh Racecourse has a great history! It has been there for 206 years.

In between the horse racing there is live singing available if you like that!

The opening times are often during midday and sometimes there are morning or night uses.

Pinkie Football Pitch
1 Linkfield Rd, Musselburgh EH21 7LN

You should go to Pinkie because it is free and has very good facilities. The people there are friendly and it's a good way to get active. You can play football, rugby, hockey and there's a track for running. They also have a huge grass pitch. There are also shops very near in case you need a drink.

It is home to Musselburgh Windsor FC. They play most Sundays, and you can come watch for free.

There's a breakfast roll van there every Sunday when the football is on.

Musselburgh Sports Centre
101 Newbigging
Musselburgh EH21 7AS

Opening times: Mon, Wed and Fri - 7am - 9:30pm, Tue and Thur - 6am - 9:30pm Sat and Sun 9am - 4:30pm

You should go to Musselburgh sports centre because there's many activities you can do such as swimming, badminton, football, basketball and squash. And there's also a gym and another for teens who want to start the gym

The prices are very cheap and the staff are very friendly. They help you if you are struggling. After swimming you can enjoy a hot sauna. Also there's a cafeteria that does pizza and drinks for when you've done your swimming.

It has a big car park. You can also get pizza and chips for £2. You can also get sweet treats and juice. There are vending machines.

It's good for high school kids at the Grammar School because it's right next door.

Section Three

The Outdoors

Experience the fresh air

Written by Connie & Zoe

River Esk

I would recommend you go to the River Esk because there is a lot to do like walking, cycling, and running. You can also feed the ducks and there is a shop about 5 minutes away. You can buy bird food in there if you want.

Along the river there is one special bridge with padlocks on it. People put them there, and it's like the one in Paris. Timpson's sell the locks and they're on High Street if you want to lock something to the bridge. People do it to remember their relationship by putting their names or initials on the padlock. They then throw the key into the river.

To get to the River Esk, you can travel on foot, by bike, by car or by bus. The bus stops are located on High Street.

The Beach and Harbour

The harbour is full of boats and you can walk around and see the views. Some people like jumping off the end into the water.

You can walk along the beach with your dog or do water sports in the sea, like wild swimming and paddleboarding. The views are really amazing. It's a sandy beach too!

There are public toilets there and also lots of parking if you're driving from out of town.

The beach and harbour has a lot to do like there's a children's sand park with a digger at the side and there are also pies that you can eat from the food van. They also sell burgers, chips, and hot dogs.

There are lots of birds, so you can sit and eat your food and watch the wildlife.

Memory and Reflection

On the beach, there is a statue of Musselburgh. In the old days, this beach and harbour was known for having a lot of mussels, so it was named Musselburgh.

The statue is 12ft high and 6ft wide and made of stainless steel. It is called Memory and Reflection. It was built by a sculptor called Michael Johnson. We really like this statue.

The Lagoons

I would recommend going to the lagoons because it is a peaceful place to take your dogs for a walk. You can also take paddleboards or canoes there. If you don't own one of these, you can still take part in the watersports there as you can hire paddlebaords and boats.

If you take bird food, you can feed the ducks and swans. Dogs are allowed in the water too for a swim, but when it's nesting season, the swans will get very protective, so you need to be careful with your dog.

When you look into the water, you can see little frogs and tadpoles.

There are picnic benches there, so you should take a picnic and sit down to relax.

The lagoons are surrounded by trees and only a 10 or 15-minute walk from the town centre.

You should go there because seeing all the wildlife is lovely and you can walk to it, but it feels different from the town.

Lewisvale Park

21 Park Gardens, Inveresk
Musselburgh EH21 7JY

Lewisvale Park is one of the parks in
Musselburgh, and we think it is the best one. It's
mostly good for children, but it's open 24 hours
a day.

The park is really big and inside there is a
walled garden with birds, and sports pitches
like cricket and tennis. There's also a bandstand

that has been there since 1900. But the park has been there way longer than that!

It's open to the public and free to go, so it's definitely worth a visit!

Section Four

Fort Kinnaird
"The Fort"

A stronghold for shoppers

Written by Jack and Andrea

Fort Kinnaird

The Fort is an outdoor shopping centre in Musselburgh. It was first opened in 1989 and has remained a perfect place for eating, shopping, watching a movie and exercising. It is open 12 hours a day Monday - Friday and between 9am - 6pm on Saturday and Sunday.

There are free restrooms as well as free parking, with over 2600 spaces. There's an outdoor play area, ATMs, lost property and baby changing facilities.

Fort Kinnaird is easy to get to as there is a bus stop right in front of Greggs.

Game

32 Newcraighall Rd
Edinburgh EH15 3RD

Game is a video game shop. They sell games and consoles. You can also sell your old games there which is good if you have finished playing with them and want to get some money.

In some places an XBox and 3 games might be £400 but in Game it would be about £250, so they're much cheaper. You can also test games out there before you buy them.

If you like games, it's the best place in the area to go!

Pets at Home

Fort Kinnaird Retail Park
Newcraighall Rd, Edinburgh
Fort Kinnaird EH15 3RD

Opening times: Mon - Fri 9am - 8pm
Sat 9am - 7pm, Sun 10am - 6pm

Pets at Home is a pet shop where you can buy food and toys for all different types of animals. You can also buy animals there: little lizards, snakes, rabbits, hamsters, guinea pigs and gerbils. They sell fish from small to medium sized, obviously not things like sharks.

The dog grooming place they have there, The Groom Room, is really good because they don't embarrass the dogs by giving them rubbish cuts. If you take your dog there, which you should, they will come out with a fresh fade

There is also a vets inside the shop, called Better Vets. They just do check-ups and small things but not operations.

In Pets at Home you can book an experience
like 'Hold an Animal' experience.

If you have got a pet you should definitely go to
Pets at Home at the Fort.

*It's really good to go in there,
but it's hard to write about it so
just go and have a look yourself.*

Five Guys

6 Kinnaird Park Fort Kinnaird
Edinburgh, EH15 3RD

Five Guys is a burger restaurant at the Fort. You can get burgers, milkshakes and chips.

When I went to Five Guys with my family, I had a delicious burger, but it was really expensive. I would go again though as it's worth it! Milkshakes are £5.25 and the burgers are £6.00 - 8.00.

The best thing there is the bacon and cheeseburger.

JD Sports

**Unit 34, Fort Kinnaird, Newcraighall Rd
Edinburgh, EH15 3HS**

**Opening times: Mon - Fri 9am - 8pm
Sat 9am - 6pm, Sun 10am - 6pm**

JD is a popular, branded clothes and shoes shop. They sell lots of different things there. Their most expensive shoe is a Nike football boot that costs £245.00.

We like to go there for football shoes. You can also get tracksuits and there are walls of shoes when you go in there.

It's really good to go in there, but it's hard to write about it so just go and have a look yourself.

McDonald's

Kinnaird Retail Park, Fort Kinnaird Shopping Newcraighall Rd, Complex EH15 3RD

McDonald's is the best place in Musselburgh because it has good food - breakfast, lunch and dinner. You can get a breakfast roll, hamburger and other stuff too!

The breakfast menu starts at 5am and finishes at 11am. And it is open 24 hours a day so you can drive and get food there when you want!

They also sell nice vegan food too, apparently. I haven't tried it because I like meat, but some people say it's really good, like the McPlant burger.

It can get really busy, but it is worth going there if you're hungry because you won't have to wait very long for food.

It is not very expensive but it can get pricey if you get a big meal. They do the Pound Saver Menu, but if you get a large burger and chips, it will be about £8.

ODEON

Fort Kinnaird Retail Park, Newcraighall Rd
Edinburgh EH15 3HP

The ODEON is a cinema! You can go there to watch a movie, but it is really expensive for a ticket, about £10. Before you go in to watch a film, you can get popcorn, sweets, hot dogs, drinks and ice cream. There is also a pick'n' mix area. But you should buy sweets before you go in because that's expensive too.

As well as movies, they show football matches like the Champions League.

If you get asked to do jury duty, you sometimes have to do it at this cinema too.

Section Five

The High Street

Grab a bite

Written by Reese and Kieran

Greggs
134 High St, Musselburgh EH21 7EA

Go to Greggs for a good breakfast, lunch or dinner. For breakfast they do bacon rolls, square sausage and sausage rolls. There is a bunch of stuff on the menu like pies, baguettes, good juices and donuts.

It's not very expensive but they are putting the sausages rolls up by 5p! The wedges are so good and they are only £1.25 and you get about 12 wedges.

Most of the staff are friendly!

You can sit in or take it away. At lunch time it is pretty busy so you might not get a table.

You should go there to get great service and food that tastes good at a cheap price.

Luca's

High St, Musselburgh, Edinburgh EH21 7AG
Opening times: Mon - Sun 9am - 10pm

Luca's is an old and famous ice cream shop. Its full name is S. Luca of Musselburgh. It's very popular because on a nice warm day people go to get ice cream, get a slushy or sit in the cafe. They have got hundreds of types of ice creams and they change them every week.

It is accessible by many buses and the stop is just outside. There is also parking nearby for probably 4 or 5 cars.

I recommend the mango sorbet ice cream!

It is a bit expensive, well maybe mid price, but it's definitely worth it! A junior ice cream cone is £2.90 or £3.40 if you want a flake too. An adult sized ice cream sundae is £6.25.

If you want to book a party there, you can do as there is a whole other level.

The staff are so nice and polite.

Rainbows

106 High St, Musselburgh EH21 7EA
Opening times: Mon - Sat 11am - 11pm
Sun 11am - 9pm

Rainbows is an old chippy with a variety of foods, sauces and drinks. It is accessible from bus stops around the corner and a few car spaces outside.

The food goes from chips to pizza to pies, fish, fried pizza, fried sausage.

You can sit in or take it away.

It's not expensive, it's about £2.50 for a big portion of chips which we think is pretty good.

Subway

131 High St, Musselburgh EH21 7DD

Opening times: Sun - Thur 9:30am - 7pm
Fri and Sat 9:30am - 8pm

Subway is a sandwich shop.
They have different subs on the menu like Italian BMT and roast chicken. We recommend you get the ham, cheese, chicken and lettuce sub with southwest sauce on Italian bread. Oh and have it toasted

When you go in you pick the bread, then the meat and then it gets toasted before you pick the salad. After that you choose a drink and a cookie.

It costs £3.50 during school hours if you have a Young Scot card.

It's usually pretty busy in there. You can sit in or take it away. It's also on Deliveroo if you want to have it delivered.

In our opinion it is better than Greggs because there is more variety of ingredients and Subway sandwiches are freshly made on the spot.

ACKNOWLEDGEMENTS

Thank you to Head Teacher Ms Hannan for inviting us into Musselburgh Grammar school for the first time. We worked with Ms Lock and Ms Roddy over 8 weeks to produce this guidebook.

A huge well done to the students at Musselburgh Grammar for their effort and enthusiasm in writing about the place they know best!

Thank you to our volunteers who work so diligently with our young people to inspire them to write and help let them believe they can produce a book! Also, our E.L.E.P.H.A.N.T volunteers work behind the scenes lightly editing the work. The wonderful cover was created by artist Ailsa Purdie who also worked on our children's book, *The Biggest Fan*.

VOLUNTEERS

Classroom

Lesley McMillan
Kevin Kempton
Amanda Ferrier

E.L.E.P.H.A.N.T

Bina Martin
Celise Downs

Cover Design and Illustration

Ailsa Purdie

The Super Power Agency is a Scottish charity (SC046550) working to improve the lives and literacy skills of Scotland's youth. Through writing workshops, creative programming and a corps of dedicated volunteers, we help to give young people in schools and community organisations the powers they need to foster aspiration, close the attainment gap in education and become successful learners and confident individuals.

FIND & FOLLOW

Website

superpoweragency.com

Instagram

@Superpoweragency

Facebook

@Superpoweragency

Twitter

@Superpow3

LinkedIn

@Superpoweragency